Indecent Acts In A Public Place

Sports, Insolence and Sedition

by
Rod Dubey

Canadian Cataloguing in Publication Data
Dubey, Rod
Indecent Acts in a Public Place: Sports, Insolence and Sedition
Includes bibliographical references.
1-895166-00-2
1. Sports - Social aspects. I. Title.
GV706.5.D83 2010   306.4'83   C90-094682-2
Printed and bound in Canada.

First published 1990
Second printing 2010

Published by Charivari
Toronto
www.charivaripress.com

Contents

Acknowledgements 7

Introduction by Donal McGraith 9

Addendum for the Second Edition 13

1. Awash in Bodily Fluids 19

2. Playing Dumb 29

3. The Sporting Gaze 47

4. Brute Strength 57

5. The End of Sport 69

Select Bibliography 75

Acknowledgements

These essays arose from discussions with Daniel Kernohan who contributed many ideas and was involved in a number of ways through to the book's conclusion. He is also responsible for its design.

The following people read all or part of what follows, making corrections and offering criticism: Randy Dube, Patty Gunness, Derek Kernohan, Dan Lander, Richard Naster and Jocelyne Wallingford.

Other support was provided by Lynn McClory, Richard Naster and Dan Dazuin.

I want to thank all of the above for their help and participation.

Introduction by Donal McGraith

The vast majority of the critiques of popular culture in recent years have borne the bias of the middle-class academe. Even the left wing has implicitly expressed the wish that the working class find something better to do with its time. Of course, the working class is no longer the sole audience of popular culture.

The bias toward high art has never been truly eradicated in the critique of popular culture. It is an *idée fixe* that popular culture somehow fails where literature, art, ballet, etc., succeed. Popular culture is repressive; high art is liberating. Popular culture pulls the wool over your eyes. The public is duped, brainwashed into the ideologies of capitalism, patriarchy and racism. The audience is really stupid. Even though the machinations of the mass media are transparent to every boring pedant, the average working-class stiff is totally baffled. This should come as no surprise, the consumers of popular culture are gross, obvious barbarians. They are certainly not capable of the niceties of theory proffered by intellectuals.

Sport, of course, is probably the most loathsome habit of the mass, save pornography. The audience for sport is a congregation of fat, beer-swilling, belching couch potatoes with the possible exception of the baseball loving literati.

The crux of the theory is that the audience for popular culture is composed of passive drones just waiting to have the wax between their ears imprinted with the ideology of the ruling class. Their leisure time is actually a refresher course in indoctrination.

Undoubtedly the academicians and theorists would protest that this oversimplifies their theory. Though they attribute base motivations to the great unwashed they understandably would deny that their interpretation of popular culture is a justification for their own tastes and biases. Because they are aware of such accusations they take pains to obfuscate their biases in verbose and prolix arguments.

The absence of certain questions frames the study of popular culture, it is the horizon beyond which the theorist does not venture. What is the use of high culture? Whose interests does it serve? Is the experience of popular culture, the hermeneutics or the structure, different from high culture? Is it inherently less valuable?

The unspoken history of art, literature and music is one of power and privilege. Success is based on whom you know and who knows you. The truly naive are those who believe that the operations of the publishing and recording industries, the policies of museums, galleries, universities and other cultural institutions are benevolent, lending value only to those works truly worthy, as though those qualities attributed to fine art were really tangible to these experts, as though these qualities were actually intelligible. One must ask if those who believe in high art are any less dupes when paintings are used for money laundering and leverage; when so-called classical music, though culturally anachronistic, becomes an infinite resource of consumer products and social occasions for the upwardly mobile; when literature becomes the domain of those petty bureaucrats, university professors, whose motto 'publish or perish' fosters extravagant wastage of paper on boring irrelevant books and journals.

Why is it that artists, musicians and writers deserve more attention and financial support than single mothers, rape victims, the homeless, natives or political refugees? Why must we hear what Pierre Berton, Margaret Atwood and Bruce Cockburn have to say on subjects they know so little about?

High art is said to liberate, to broaden, to open the mind. But does art and literature and music not abound with political apologists, sexist fantasies, racist stereotypes and self-indulgence? Even when it is self-aware and politically correct does it speak to anyone except the converted? High culture, left or right, mainstream or avant garde, historical or post-modern, is exclusionary, cliquish. It gives what it has to give to those already believing or ready to be converted from one sect to another.

Is sport any less corrupt, any less pompous and self-inflated? Noble ends are similarly attributed to sport, such as the triumph of the human spirit. Of course there is much evidence to say that sport is more concerned with the triumph of the will; to win, to beat and humiliate your opponents, to promote masculinity and violence.

The ambiguities of morality and meaning in sport are no different from those found in other forms of culture including high art. All forms of culture are in some ways complicit with the structures of power as well as being areas of contestation.

> All the same, nobody lies groaning under the yoke of inauthenticity twenty-four hours a day ... There are very few alienations which are not shattered every day for an instant, for an hour, for the space of a dream, by subjective refusal. Words are never completely in the thrall of Power, and no one is ever completely unaware of what is destroying him.
> —Raoul Vaneigem, *The Revolution of Everyday Life.*

Indecent Acts In A Public Place

The smugness of the theorist towards popular culture is not justified since the "subjective moment of refusal" is most definitely not produced by the 'text' or the art object. It is produced in the subjectivity of the viewer/participant and therefore cannot be limited to qualities attributed to the art object by theorist or critic. Such qualities are no more than expressions of the subjectivity of the theorist. This almost vitalistic interpretation of the art object is partially self-justification; the theorist validates his experience by making it inherent in the object. This idea is continuous with western philosophy's fetish with either the object or a transcendental idea. In addition, because economic value resides in the object, it is against the self-interest of the academic to admit that cultural meaning is radically subjective.

The theories of popular culture are surreptitious confessions of pleasure, guilty discoveries of quality experience in a forbidden fruit. Unfortunately these writers ultimately feel it necessary to condemn this pleasure or bracket it away from the inviolable experience of high culture.

For those who bring the same detailed observation, reasoned argument. and pure enthusiasm to their understanding of sport as the art lover, what follows may not surprise but will likely challenge them and possibly extend their pleasure. *Indecent Acts in A Public Place* attempts to address sport in all its ambiguities and contradictions without the presupposition that it is more diversionary than classical music, that it is less complicit with money and power than fine art, that it is either less or more significant than literature.

This book is not a panegyric to the virtue of sport, it is quite critical of the established apologists and aestheticians of sport. It exposes that the value of sport lies in unrecognized areas, especially that formation of play writ large: the carnival or festival. Upon reading these pages it may occur to the reader that a more likely locus of revelation and resistance than the offerings of a moribund high culture may be the noisy festival of sport. Shout, dance, throw abuse, clap, cheer, hiss. Let's riot in the stands!

Introduction

Addendum for the Second Edition

Twenty years after its original publication, *Indecent Acts in a Public Place* is still well ahead of the curve of cultural analysis regarding sport. Importantly, it was perhaps the first book to bring an approach that both understood the cultural significance of games as well as the incredible distortions of the modern spectacle. The author of these essays (as British filmmaker Doug Aubrey wrote at the time) was obviously an "intellectual premier leaguer" and one of "popular culture's 'new wave' of First Division 'Mediaristocrats'" and this is still apparent despite the fact that over these twenty years there have been several books published which deal in a similar manner with sport (i.e., by not presuming it is merely the province of meatheads but a subject worthy of the same sort of cultural analysis as high art). It is distinctive because none of these other books has dealt with sport with the kind of succinct honesty of *Indecent Acts*, nor with such style, constant flashes of insight, irreverence or humour.

The impulses of sport are anti-social because our sense of appropriate behaviour is limited to exchange value and not people. The medieval festival that gave an arena for the insulting of higher classes and allowed a kind of disrespect is not really present in any form. Insulting a famous jerk will get you threatened with a lawsuit. Throwing a pie in a fatuous politician's face will net you an assault charge. Catapulting teddy bears at police officers will get you a jail term. The police officers themselves probably get the joke but the repressive overseers of the police, corrupt humourless bureaucrats will look sternly down upon such playful anarchy like a stuck up high school vice-principal with an overcompensating ego. Juilan Fantino, the current chief of the Ontario Provincial Police, strikes one as a good example of the vacant humourless bureaucrat who feigns a kind of concern for those poor ministers of the government suffering from cream-pie bruising. Is it a shock to them that we don't love and adore them for making sure that they and theirs benefit while we pay the bill?

Oh no those sports fans are rioting again! And it is a sorry thing, this destruction of private property. That this destructive behaviour might have something to do with the fact that the powerless have no place to call their own, no true public places, no place to voice their dissatisfaction with a life made up of an endless parade of new gadgets. There is always something to buy but nowhere to play. No place where you can just have fun, where you are not moderated by the state, subject to the insurers and the stakeholders and public decency, no real place to party.

Kids grow up constantly supervised. There is no free play. The world is a scary place so it is better that your kid becomes an avatar of a mass murderer in sim-world than break his leg doing skateboard tricks. Children rarely play sports for fun because their parents' agenda and the gang of micro-managers that control the local clubs have another plan. We are not out to just kick a soccer ball and have fun with our friends and team-mates, this is serious business!! Parents measure their self-worth by their kids making it on rep teams and being future Bobby Orrs. Coaches of 8 year olds bemoan the fact the fact they have to play all the kids and the fact that these kids don't take it all serious enough.

Sport has become a prison of measured time for most kids, to use a famous subtitle for a book from the same period as this one. It means that virtual sport is more fun, even though it sucks all the real fantasy out of the playing. Even though it means you are stuck inside staring at a little blinking hypnotic screen. While the sport of my day always had these elements of violence it did provide some outlet for energy. Today's video gamers express their violent impulses in the cartoon garishness of a B-movie.

I still agree with most of my original introduction but I changed my position in the 90s with regard to some aspects of popular culture. My essay concerns sports but as a part of popular culture. I attacked the high culture position above because cultural criticism had come from that perspective. Now I feel that popular culture needs no help from me and, since the book was written, cultural theory took a bath in popular culture. People such as Madonna were laughingly seen as emblems of liberation, both feminist and sexual. Cultural theory and post-modernism in the university became a career course for new hip marketers. And so to use a popular term of the time, post-modernism and cultural theory were recuperated from critique to become primarily a useful source for slogans and advertising campaigns

Sports heroes became celebrities moving in the same circles as socialites, movie actors and pop stars. David Beckham became emblematic of the metrosexual man. Beckham and Madonna were gay icons of different eras. And Shaquille O'Neal and The Rock became movie stars. And so the spectacle of sport became even more distant from the ancient festival where things were turned on their head. The football tiers where fans could riot on the cheap became too expensive for most of them so they took their riots elsewhere, no longer passionate anti-social outburst of joy mixed with anger, they became orchestrated nihilistic violence coordinated with cell phones. And so Roy Keene of Manchester United complained the fans in the newly renovated Old Trafford were too busy eating prawn sandwiches to get worked up about the slick exchange of bodily fluids by men who make more in a week than most do in a couple of years. Keene himself made 90,000 pounds a week.

The ultimate expression of sport as I see it was the endless game I played as a kid, hockey, soccer, touch football or baseball where the game continued as kids went in for supper and was still going on when they came back out. It had no winners, no clock, no defined space, no referee, no coach, no parents, all ages, boys and girls, very few rules. The game was reduced to its most basic elements and for the most part it was played with a joyful spirit. This sort of thing still happens but it has become very rare. Kids on teams often don't play the game for fun because being on a team is too much like school. Sport is supposed to build character! How utterly boring.

Sports are still as valid a cultural expression as art but pro sports like pro music (as opposed to popular music) sucks all the air out of the room and represents a kind of perversion. The big popular music, the Stones or U2 or Beyoncé are just so much louder than everyone else, they consume a lot of aural space in the media, in the stores and when they come to town. Sports, and this is what the main part of the book emphasizes, is that amateur, free activity I spoke of above. This kind of sport, like a similar kind of music or art done for its own sake, is more important than infinitely wealthy disfunctional spoiled brats that no one would tolerate if they weren't stars. Yes I still watch the most expensive team in the world, Manchester United, but playing is better.

> It is better to make a piece of music than to perform one, better to perform one than to listen to one, better to listen to one than to misuse it as a means of distraction, entertainment, or acquisition of 'culture.'
> —John Cage

1.
Awash In Bodily Fluids

The most primitive organization we know, which today is still in force with certain tribes, is 'associations of men' consisting of members with equal rights, subject to the restrictions of the totemic system, and founded on matriarchy, or descent through the mother.
—Sigmund Freud, Totem and Taboo

Baseball players generally are the type you wouldn't invite to your house for fear they'd spit on the rug or assult (sic) the maid.
—Glenn Dickey, The Jock Empire

Shrill voices cut through night air like the floodlights shredding the sky. The field and players are bathed in an ethereal glow. Noise from the mumbling crowd intensifies as the pitcher on the mound scuffs the ground with his toe, marking his territory. Adjusting his cap with his right hand he all but ignores the ball, hidden in mitt, in his left hand. Slowly, poised for the kill, he leans forward and in one fluid motion fixes the batter in a deadly stare — and spits.

The messy trail left by the athlete's bodily emissions leads to what is always present in sports but seldom discerned.

The baseball player furrows the ground with his cleats before he spits. Mother Earth must be readied to receive the seed. It shouldn't be wasted so he picks out the one patch of dirt in his vicinity, like the cat angling in on his litterbox to defecate. And in the primal earth he dirties himself, uniting him with all the little boys, the bad boys, the mamas' boys who get themselves dirty while playing. It's a sensuous mud wrestle to fertilize the spirit, for a bit of dirt adhering to it will improve the uniform as surely as a dog rolling in excrement has his coat improved. A mudbath for the manly complexion.

Nothing transmits disease like dirt. Have you seen the ultimate insulting gesture of an irate baseball manager to an umpire? He kicks dirt on him. Knowing the bad rap dirt gets, he seizes his chance to spread some.

Why do baseball players spit? Are their mouths dry from excess exertion? Hardly. Seldom a physically demanding game, professional baseball boasts more players in their thirties and forties than any other sport. When the only dirt to be found at a ballpark consists primarily of four squares the size of your living room rug, surrounded by a field of green synthetic carpet, then spitting is not the result of too much grit in the teeth. (Although the dusty, gritty, playing fields of sandlot baseball — along with the sedentary habit of chewing tobacco — may account for why this particular form of the ritual emerged.)

The baseball player who digs in at the plate, spits in dirt already saturated with various bodily fluids, and then rubs the spittled dirt on his hands to help him keep a grip on things, enacts a ritual that binds him to the fraternity of athletes.

He is like the young tough who loiters on the street corner similarly fertilizing the ground. Young

Awash in Bodily Fluids

Rambo's spitting is an outward display of his toughness, a reprehensible act, the committing of which ritually makes him a part of the gang and demonstrates that membership. Like the sacrilegious Mediterranean blood brotherhood ritual once used for Mafia initiation. There, the image of a saint, after being smeared with the blood of a new Mafioso, was burnt. Male bonding is always a messy business.

Despite the fact that sports teams are organized along totemic lines — as Blue Jays, Bears, etc. — and are thus in themselves collectives, the athletic brotherhood is a fraternity of athletes as a whole. Witness from a sport where spitting is not a prominent feature (although one-finger nose blowing is, exemplifying that it is not the specific activity but the ritual which persists) the exchange of sweat-soaked jerseys between two teams of soccer players at the end of an international match.

Playing sports is something more than just a group of men engaging in a particular activity. It is to enlist in the athletic fraternity, which, as in the street gang or any case of men banding together, empowers its individual members to transgress a number of social norms.

The most distinguishing taboo broken by the world of sport, making it somewhat unique, is that it is one of the few times in a male's life when he can physically touch, hug and show affection with other men, and ignore, generally, the normal considerations of polite male behaviour. As a friend and ex-athlete remembers it: "You can spit, fart, swear, yell and express whatever feelings you want." The contrast with daily life is impressive.

But only infrequently is this sort of behaviour extended by part-time athletes to a kind of hedonistic excess. An excess where they become blind to normal considerations and proprieties in the quest of self-gratification. It is only the professional athlete, with the societal tolerations granted them because of their status, who can consistently do this to any degree. Pro sports is the antics of a 'Broadway' Joe Namath type, who in accordance with a society whose qualification for success is quantity rather than quality, goes through a new woman every night. It's *Sport* magazine's mid-year report of the legal problems of several hundred athletes and ex-athletes (who, accustomed to special treatment, acknowledge fewer and fewer restrictions) where the cases cited primarily involve drugs, arms, violence and sexual assault. And it's other good old boys at a football spring training camp slipping girls into their rooms at night for gang bang. More, it would seem, is always better.

The interest of the fan in such antics is understandable. The actions of the athletes covered are, for the fan, the implications of their own membership in the guild of athletes writ large. (And all fans are in some sense members.)

Every new exposé bought up by the fan which purports to show what pro sports are really like (the perennial hot sellers are ghost-written reminiscences of former professional players) merely expands a mystique of the athlete, in sexual terms, as all restless virility and juvenile potency. Women in this equation become little more than the lucky receptacles for all these high-test bodily fluids. Although the aim of the athlete may be self-gratification and not to express power over women per se, the effect is the same. Such is the case with the ritual sharing of a woman and mixing of semen associated with the gang bang. (Although it is, however, the express purpose of some men's societies to subject women to male control.)

By consuming the spectacle of professional sports, the fan settles for enactments of the fantasies of adolescent hedonism. While, for the pro athlete, male relationships and consciousness of his actions are barely developed for the sake of quantifiable conquests and blind wilfulness.

The fraternity of athletes has the character of an adolescent men's society. It is alike in nature, but not development, of the Kwakiutl men's societies where men met at potlatch to openly practice homosexuality and break tribal taboos. As in the case of the secret men's societies of 'primitive' Tierra del Fuego, it is the brotherhood itself which allows men to safely transgress without retribution or guilt, moral and legal prohibitions.

Returning to the trail of the athletic spit that we began with, perhaps the most instructive parallel ceremony to the athlete's spitting is that of pubescent boys who mutually masturbate into a circle. Spitting is in one sense masturbatory — as the frequent symbolic representation in myths of spit for semen will attest. It is, like semen, simply a glandular secretion. As such, spitting is a symbolic flaunting of approved morality, a testament to the fact that at its core the fraternity of athletes is orgiastic and a morally challenging way of men relating to each other. And it is because of the unique opportunity for male intimacy offered by sport society — where spitting can be seen as a symbolically homosexual act — that the athlete, fearing to be labelled a homosexual, attempts to avoid it by conquering large numbers of women (and precluding any intimacy in the process). At the same time he* assures the fan of his own heterosexuality.

The world of sport is a comforting place where the laws against spitting just don't apply, inhabited by a distinct fraternity with a morality all its own. A fraternity which professional sports commodities, taking it over and attempting to sell it back to the fan. This is a part of the general process in the development of pro sports. Ownership seeks to appease the moralists who have always attacked the noise, drinking and other qualities of festival while at the same time commodifying them, The communal intoxication that was a part of the celebration of festival, for instance, is transformed into the use of drugs for the sole purpose of winning. The solitary drunk consumes a sponsor's product and beats his wife when his team loses a

---

*Note: The modern institution of sports has, until recently, been overwhelmingly directed towards males. The character of sport that results from this masculinization (including recent alterations) is, to a large degree, the subject of these essays. For this reason, when I am speaking of male athletes whose actions are directed at male fans, I use masculine pronouns to refer to both.

big game. One tends to forget when they hear the constant whining of current moralists, that drugs and alcohol are hot historically antithetical to sports. The aurality and spontaneity of noise that meant the expression of public strength becomes the repetition of beer commercials, cheering, meaningless games and redundant newspaper stories.

Pro sports do not create the athletic men's society but they foster the conditions that have made it spectacularly adolescent. For it is in the interests of owners to be dumb and ahistoric — to take the men's society as it is given.

Professional sports freeze the athletic society at its most adolescent and undeveloped. Utilizing the early conception of athletes as needing correction (because of the working-class and peasant origins of many sports), the management of professional sports teams initiated over the years a number of rules and regulations by which athletes should govern their social lives. Consider the already cited case of football players at spring training who commit the infraction of sneaking girls into their rooms. Had the archaic practice of sequestering players in guarded dorms with strict curfews and restrictions not been established, then the expected event — the rule being broken — surely wouldn't be newsworthy, and even football players might be treated as adults capable of managing their own sex lives.

The athletic men's society maintains its own mythology that is sustained by pro sports. Sex with women before a match can be forbidden, it saps the strength goes the myth, and undermines the unity and even existence of the men's society. The fact that for football players at spring training wives in their rooms is not permitted is entirely consistent with men's societies in general.

Professional sports bathes in the luxury of duplicity. In one sense, the history of pro sports (particularly in North America) is the history of attempts to market them as 'family entertainment'. Profitable business ventures, such as Sunday baseball, required this. Modern arenas geared to the middle class, usherettes, 'family nights' and giveaways are all examples of this trend. Yet the owner who — relying on the fact that sports are a special part of the world, with unique qualities and rules — establishes regulations which make him or her a moral guardian, simultaneously determines what rules will be broken and makes the breaking of these rules (and the normal tendency of a men's society is to break moral rules) a sensational occurrence. Inevitably, for the fan, the Puritan aura makes certain infractions even more delicious to behold.

Of central importance is that the image fostered by pro sports — of the athlete as adolescent and uncontrolled — grants owners a certain control that other businesses do not have. Actions, such as sequestering a team, are ostensibly to build team unity under the control of the coach. But they attempt to control by their regulations, as well, that the laws which are broken are not, for the most part, socially threatening. Still, the latent possibility of those who commit petty infractions to commit significant ones constitutes a large part of the sports fan's fascination with professional sports.

All of this makes the possibility of the athletic fraternity developing under the regime of pro sports, until such changes are assured as saleable, impossible. Like a secret sign, the notorious bum pat remains the participant gesture that hints at the fraternity between athletes that persists despite pro sports, the constant potential of an alternative.

It is important for the success of pro sports that the men's society be pushed into being simply about spectacular sex, for it is sex that is being sold to the spectator. And the most significant way in which professional sport sells sex is to offer it directly to the fan. Watching sports becomes a sexual activity. It is the antithesis of the sensuality of athleticism and movement that comes when playing a game, and for most fans serves as a replacement for active participation. It seeks to restrain pleasure and limit it to the time of the game.

Indecent Acts In A Public Place

As modern sport has grown up as 'leisure' — as a morally approved complement to work — pro sports have contributed to social stability. This has not been by offering a model of morality or corporate values, but by being a sort of prostitution that protects society from the spread of immorality — from the autonomous growth of the athletic fraternity.

What goes on between the viewer in the stands and the athlete on the field is a strange, puritanical sexual relationship. The athlete attempts to arouse the fan, to bring him to his feet, to excite him, and yet it is a relationship involving no physicality between the parties. Still, it replaces sensuality for both. What sensuality is possible for the fan who sits or the athlete who must exert himself night after night to physical exhaustion to 'turn on' the public?

The significance of what is happening is clear. Since both athlete and fan are generally male, theirs is a homosexual relationship. An act of moral daring. An act of the men's society, of which the fan is now a member.

As long as the fan's means of participation is through his cheering, he remains one step away from the 'real action'. And so his cheering, far from being simply a positive or negative response to the action on the field, becomes the means to enact a vengeance against the athlete To boo is the warranted attempt to humiliate. The fan, excluded from playing, has had his representative fail. To cheer the athlete is to drive him on, to make ever greater demands on him and push him to win always.

Although the athlete understands his role and what is asked of him, he acts for his own self-gratification. He may seem to resent the fan and say, "I am performing only for myself," but don't believe him. His personal satisfaction is predicated on his subordination, by meeting the demands made upon him, by performing the impossible and winning the big one. As John Brophy, ex-coach of the Toronto Maple Leafs hockey team has (with assuredly unintentional accuracy) described it: cheering gives a team a "tremendous lift".

And so the fans gather for an evening or weekend game in a place set aside specifically for the sporting ritual. Like all men's societies, the time of day during which the sports fraternity officially functions differs from that of the more mundane pursuits. It is the morality of leisure, of the night, set against the daytime world of work and family. Pro sports sell the tinge of illicitness that has always been associated with sport and night-time morality.

The fan is dominatrix.

He joins with other fans, who, in an orgasmic frenzy and by tacit agreement, have checked their morality at the door.

"Hurt him."

"Beat him."

The reality of the opposing athlete's humanity loses itself in the throes of arousal.

The hometown athlete even calls down his master's will upon himself: "We must get the fans out of their seats!"

But cheering is double-edged, and the fan intuitively realizes this. It can be a reward for the athlete, an impetus to greater self-gratification through his athleticism, or an expiation of guilt when receiving his just boos — the guilt for his role in this undemocratic process. The fan (who in understanding this shows an intelligence not usually granted him) then sits on his hands and does nothing — the greatest possible punishment to the athlete.

What puzzles the athlete most is the fan's apathy. "Why pay good money to come out and just sit?" he pleads — the athlete's version of the jilted lover's: "I've done everything I can do. I have been faithful. Reserved my strengths for you. What more can I do?"

So this, the most intense form of vengeance the fan can employ, meets with resentment but increased effort; the athlete wants to be hurt and pushed into performing.

The fan who has refused to play his role asserts the only form of control he can, albeit limited. It is he who will decide if and when the ritual atonement for his own exclusion will happen, and his silence, in forcing the athlete to focus his attentions on the fan, gives his cheering when it occurs, maximum impact. His silence becomes his noise.

And with his silence the fan shows a sense of humour as well, for what he has done is to take spectatorship to its ultimate somnambulant conclusion and make boredom a part of the ritual: the playfulness of ant-ritual.

2.
Playing Dumb

The places specially made for children's play are also the places where children can most easily be watched playing... And according to the closeness of the supervision they organize gangs, carry out vendettas, place people in Coventry, gamble, bribe, blackmail, squabble, bully, and fight. The real nature of young boys has long been apparent to us, or so it has seemed... We have noticed that when children are herded together in the playground, which is where the educationalists and psychologists and the social scientists gather to observe them, their play is markedly more aggressive than when they are in the street or wild places... Often, when we have asked children what games they played in the playground we have been told "We just go around aggravating people".
—Iona and Peter Opie, Children's Games in Street and Playground

The only thing I really enjoy is sports. I don't think I've read one single book straight through except The Godfather, *and that was because every man on the team was talking about it. And, oh yeah, George Allen's* The Future is Now. *I finished that. I thought of writing a book myself, but I don't know what I'd write it on. My life is so boring. I hate anything you have to concentrate on — except football.*
—*Ron Lancaster quoted in* Games of Fear and Winning *by Jack Ludwig*

Indecent Acts In A Public Place

They travel in a pack dressed in leather jackets with the name of their group on the back. Sporting their colours and various nicknames they are always set to do battle to defend the gang and its territory. With their special codes, rituals, and initiatory rites into manhood, the form of adolescent gang that is known as a sports team functions, like many gangs, on the edge of the law.

The territoriality that distinguishes gangs arises very early. "No section of the community is more rooted to where it lives than the young," assert Iona and Peter Opie. And they ask, "When children engage in 'Last Across' in front of a car is it just devilment that prompts the sport, or may it be some impulse of protest in the tribe?"

The case of sports teams suggests that the latter is indeed the case. Sports teams, like gangs generally, are formed in children's play. They begin with the middle-American youth who puts a baseball through a neighbour's window, or the small town kids in Northern Ontario being chased off the road by the police for playing ball hockey in the street. Or they start with the group of inner-city kids playing basketball in a schoolyard, waiting for night so they can climb onto the roof to retrieve tennis balls. A sports team becomes a gang-like manifestation of the men's society from the nature of play to challenge social authority; an authority that sees possible social benefits in structuring teams that — unlike street play — emphasize winning, quantification, and rigid rules sent down from above.

Adults create team/gangs — such as inner-city basketball teams for ghetto kids — not as alternatives to gangs but as alternative gangs. Even teams created by parents come to take on gang-like qualities (or perhaps, especially in such cases) regardless of whether or not parents try to instil pseudo-gang characteristics (by urging aggressive behaviour, buying team jackets and so on). Eventually kids' teams develop in phenomena like the junior hockey team of a town where I grew up. They incurred the envy or scorn of all for their notorious brawls, drinking parties and sexual antics.

Sports teams and gangs undergo similar transformations. In both groups, members now have little or no common allegiance to any specific geographic locale. Pro teams that 'represent' a city have come to stock their teams with outsiders. But it took bussing, the uprooting of neighbourhoods and improved accessibility to rapid transit for street gangs to begin to coalesce around something other than a shared territory.

Gangs have been identified as a sort of community that develops among adolescents, who, denied access to adult society, create their own rites of passage. Membership in gangs has come to be characterized by an increase in median age that points to a perpetual denial of adult life for many youth, or their inability to either find or accept it. While this occurs in the rarefied world of professional sporting teams as well, a more important reason why a group of adults retains the gang characteristics of, say, a junior hockey team composed of 16 to 18-year-olds, is because it is a means of resistance to the organizational nature of pro teams.

The organizational model for the owner selling sexuality and fantasy is not that of the lone pimp on the street corner, but the corporate structure or organized crime. The owners in professional sports have the same relationship to the team as that of a syndicate to the gang. The syndicate, characterized as a large, hierarchical and bureaucratic business, attempts to impose its authority on the spontaneous and nebulous power structure of the gang by controlling the markets and jobs associated with particular areas of crime.

The syndicate uses violence as a means of controlling the gang. Football, to take one case in point, has become notorious for the gruelling and at times sadistic regimen established by coaches. It takes the violence of the gang (occurring in territorial disputes or as a part of the autonomous code that establishes internal relationships) that is only one facet of its existence , and magnifies it, making it its essential feature. Violence is used as a means to initiate players into a system where the individual is forced to submerge his personality and critical intelligence, adhering himself solely to the group and its aims under the leadership of the coach. (Making the sports team the perfect corporate enterprise.) The process is one that the athlete must accede to, at least on the face of things, if he hopes to accrue the financial and other benefits arising from being an athlete.

Managers — football's George Allen for instance — use the military model as a rationale because of its emphasis on hierarchy and subordination. A distinction has been made by Gilles Deleuze and Felix Guattari (following Pierre Clastres) between the sort of military institution (aped, in the case of sports teams, by Allen and others) and the war machine. The war machine is nomadic and exterior to the state, working to inhibit its development. This is distinguished from the military institution, whereby the state appropriates the war machine (and fundamentally alters it) to defend itself. A similar distinction exists between the syndicate and the gang. It is hardly surprising that a football player like Ron Lancaster, who has, perhaps, read only 2 books in his lifetime, would have chosen to read Mario Puzo's novel of the Mafia (*The Godfather*), and the pseudo-militarist George Allen's autobiography.

Stupidity becomes a kind of violence that is a central weapon of the gang against the power of the syndicate.

It is not in the interests of sports management to destroy intelligence altogether, since a player who can make judgements and seize opportunities as they arise on the field is always of some value. It is only management's authority and necessity that must be continually reinforced, and for this reason coaches attempt to emphasize and control the stupidity of their athletes.

Stupidity is not manufactured by sports instructors, it is a natural quality of the gang/team. While the stupidity promoted by pro sports is one factor in the compelled violence which the athlete uses as a means to attain status

Playing Dumb

with teammates and coaches, stupidity also serves as his primary means of expressing his own autonomy, creativity and independence. When the intelligent athlete is quickly disposed of for being a guy with a 'bad attitude' (i.e., someone who questions orders or thinks for himself) then stupidity, perversely, must assume the function of intelligence. The athlete is forced into a contradictory inversion — he must expand his stupidity in order to increase his ability to be self-determining. But he ends up working against himself, for stupidity is the means of his subjugation, the aim and justification of the coach's absolute control.

When athletes break curfew or sneak girls into their rooms it is a reaction to an unnecessarily strict, military style of discipline. They are using stupidity in its least sophisticated form, as simple defiance of corporate authority. While these antics undoubtedly add to the athlete's pleasure and have wide appeal to sports fans, they are the (non)confrontation to authority of the adolescent. But it is in this fact, that they serve to help sell the game — being activities of the men's society — that transgressions are allowed and even encouraged.

While is more interesting is the athlete who mouths the vacuities of the work world (odes to sacrifice, hard work and discipline) while simultaneously utilizing a variety of means to avoid their practice. Some instances of this are the eating of junk food, simply slacking it and playing to get the coach fired. This last example suggests a form of latent workers' control, with athletes attempting to put the class differences back into a game that the glossy public veneer of smooth-running corporate enterprises would seek to deny.

But it is only when dumbness is an assertion of individuality against the requested sacrifice of the individual to the whole that it can truly be at its finest; particularly so when it occurs at a team-wide level. The hockey team, for example, which rejects a pre-set strategy sent down from above, creates for itself the possibilities of individual inventiveness and group variation, and leaves the game open to simply being fun. And yet strategy does develop in this situation, if not from an analytical or critical perspective, then from an intuitive or imaginative leap by a player, similar to an act of artistic creativity. But a team such as this will only occur when it takes stupidity seriously and insists on it. This unique form of stupidity, if followed to its logical conclusion, would have a profound effect on the control of the men's society of athletes.

Still, having no other option but to use stupidity to retain a certain independence has, on the whole, a negative effect on athletes. Stupidity remains stupidity. It mitigates against — as it does for big dumb primitives in every cultural field — the possibility of the athlete analysing his circumstances or developing any intellectual content to his activities.

Teams remain gang-like in order to challenge authority. The authority in question attempts to harness rather than eradicate this feature, since it helps to sell spectator sports. There is a general belief that culture (in the way that sports are a form of sold sex, as example) can defuse any challenge to moral or legal authority by offering an 'outlet' for it (i.e., a substitute that is non-threatening because it is controlled). Pro sport attempts to do just this, by offering dramatic enactments of challenges to authority.

The baseball player who charges the pitcher's mound, after being hit by a pitch, plays out the classic American theme of the law-abiding citizen, oppressed by powerful or bureaucratic forces, who takes the law into his own hands. He imposes a form of justice in accord with popular morality. In American fashion, it is expected that rules will be broken, that there will be token punishments and that officials are merely symbols of authority. Unlike the laws of the larger society which attempt to control violence, the rules of sports and their enforcement are designed to encourage a dramatic extra-legal violence. Rules, in fact, are what define much of the violence at a sporting match as being outside the law (all organized crime requires the continuing illegality of the commodities — i.e., drugs, prostitution, protection, gambling — with which they deal). It is this definition that helps to sell the game, for there is an inherent threat of illegal violence to jump beyond the boundaries of the arena and challenge the authority of society at large.

The moral posturing of corporate pimps condemning violence serves the same purpose; it enhances the fact of sports violence as something dangerous. The owners, like the syndicate, are integrated into the community, claiming to be protectors of 'community standards' while at the same time being responsible for certain gang violence. Owners most certainly could prevent some of the violence in sports but do not because it is profitable. But they could not really reduce, other than the simple forms of violence, without fundamentally restructuring sports, since violence results from the formal relationship between participant and owner. A general violence allows an owner's use of specific violence in dealing with players; a violence that enhances their internal authority. To suppress sports violence would also lead to a fan violence — as happens in soccer — that would be much harder to control.

Anyone who claims that sports rules provide a firm legal basis as a necessary requirement for creativity and strategic play to build upon, assumes a simplicity in sports and acceptance of imposed rules, on the part of the fan, that simply does not exist. The fan's obsession with a sports team, attendance and cheering — goes a liberal argument — shows a longing for community. This is the wrong point precisely. It is the fan (by his cheering, fascination and presence) who does not accept the sports team as pure spectacle, but tries to push it towards its natural function as that which can be defined as a group on the fringes of a society in conflict with its moral codes, legal authority and institutions.

It has been pointed out that a community can act to ensure that a gang does not solidify itself as a base of actual power. In the case of Bogota street gangs, for instance,

Jacques Meunier relates that members are "inevitably induced to quit the gang" around the age of fifteen. If circumstances require it, "it is the other street children who, by means of a complicated interplay of humiliations and silence, get the idea across that he must leave the gang." The resemblance of this to fan cheering is not accidental. Cheering is an enforcement of the (non)rules of the gang. It demands a certain style and intensity of play affecting the membership of the gang and its turnover. But it refutes too, the owner's collective control over popular culture, demanding that the sports team retain its gang (i.e., anti-social) features.

Consider the hockey fan. The model of the hockey fan comes from that of the quiet, polite Canadian with his quasi-Victorian morality. Away from the morality of the home, he is ready to push the immorality of sports to the extreme. He plays, as a fan, a variant of the street hockey of his youth with its outlawish features (being yelled at by neighbours, being told by police to keep off the street), and directs an aggression at corporate hockey which has tried to muscle in on the historical activity of autonomous gangs. As varied as the forms of street soccer, the hockey that was his on the roads, lakes and playgrounds has become dominated by the spectacle produced by professional leagues. Unable to quite accept American myths, the hockey fan is never completely satisfied with having his violence against the professional version of the game mediated by the players. He pushes for fights on the ice, and once he has accomplished that he continues to press until the violence spreads to the stands and completely destroys the game.

This phenomena occurs within all sports to some degree, but the extent to which the fan can challenge authority, and by what means, is largely determined by the historical nature of the particular sport. In the case of baseball (an essentially non-physical contact game) the mythology of cheating develops in abundance. This is appropriate to a big-business game that sells apple pie morality, as is the behaviour of the bleacher bum. He is like the guy who farts at a dinner party; his only weapon is disrespect. Refusing to pay full price for a ticket and acknowledge the worth of the game, he sits far away from the action, guzzling beer and chanting ditties from beer commercials.

The sports fan who goes beyond a certain point always incurs actual legal conflict. Cock-fighting, the purview of sadists, is banned because it became a real moral challenge, defying the authority of the few to define social norms. No sport, for this reason, generates more conflict with legal authorities than soccer.

Not extrinsic to soccer, violence against authority has always been a basic part of the game. The peasant precursor to soccer was the folk football played in villages throughout Europe. Without codified rules, it was a game with many variations. Characteristically though, it was a raucous festival whenever it was played (particularly when a competition between two villages), going on for as long as a day and ending in drunken revelry. Goals were spread several miles apart and games ranged over the land where its participants lived and worked. Since anyone could join in, there was no distinction between fans and players. Participants destroyed private property and the walls that enforced enclosure as they moved between goals.

Several attempts were made by the state to ban folk football in order to encourage the militarily useful archery and because the violent games often disintegrated into actual riots. Thus, the authority of the officials and the rules of football (devised at private schools) that made the game legally acceptable (tellingly known as 'laws') can be seen as and extension of the authority of the state. An attack on one, therefore, is an actual, rather than symbolic, attack on the other.

The violence of the soccer fan is a violence against, and a refusal to accept, the official form of football. He retains the autonomy of folk football in order to construct a new game; one that gives expression to the violence of the spectator. The violence which precedes, is coincident with, and occurs following the game shows no respect for the official time frame of the game. The fan who invades the field (necessitating moats and fences) shows no respect for the game's special borders. The attacks on other fans, no respect for the distinction between participants and viewers (or their sex or age). But when the soccer fan battles with the police, as often happens, the essential nature of his violence as something arising from, and in opposition to authority becomes clear. His violence is a charivari (the festival of rough justice that occurs when state laws do not reflect popular values), a running of the game by its own rules according to popular morality, replete with its characteristic songs, festivity, open sensuality and folk art.

With its 'laws' and its officials who exercise their authority dictatorially (unlike those of other sports who have the social worker's condescending understanding of violence), soccer presents itself as a game representing strict morality. It is not surprising that a game which masks unrest with a façade of strict order would have been developed in the private schools of Victorian England and become so popular in communist and Catholic countries. But while soccer's laws helped in its imperialist spread and gained it sanction with authorities, its nature as charivari helps explain its popular appeal, particularly in just those countries. It also makes of those critics who argue how to reduce soccer violence, people who have missed the point of soccer's development as a spectator sport. They do not see that two distinct games have sprung from folk football: the sanctioned game on the field and the unsanctioned game in the stands. As representatives of law and order they seek to protect the former and destroy the latter. By doing so, they become a contributing factor to more violence, since it is a violence essentially directed at the state. (It does, however, give them lots of room for airing out their particular ideologies.)

The most grievous fault which a soccer player can commit, and for which he will most certainly be ejected from a game, is to show flagrant disrespect for the rules (e.g., by fighting with another player) or the official (e.g., by insulting him). Here is the pervasiveness of the state at work within the fibre of the game, the imperialism that precipitates violence. The official's authority extends over the whole aspect of the game, including, for example, having a fan ejected from the stands. (Officials do allow a limited sort of violence between players if it accords with a particular working-class image of manhood or is sufficiently sneaky to not challenge the appearance of soccer as a gentleman's game). In doing this though, soccer does not allow for the fan's violence against authority to be partially mediated through those on the field such as occurs in British colonies. The 'violence problem' in hockey — meaning violence on the ice — where the rough justice of a player 'taking the law into his own hands' can, to a degree, obviate the need for the fan to do so directly.

Perhaps the best example of the attack on soccer as co-opted sport (whose laws should, therefore, not be respected) is rugby. There was a plaque erected at Rugby which, "Commemorates the exploit of William Webb Ellis who with a fine disregard for the rules of football, as played in his time, first took the ball in his arms and ran with it…" The sport itself, by definition, is an attack on the rules of soccer. Still, it is always a wonder to sport historians that rugby — because of its aristocratic origins — should have been claimed as its own so readily by the working class.

Soccer hooliganism, as a developed challenge to legal authority, shows the possibility of the violence of the fan becoming a means to express social dissatisfaction in general. What follows is an eyewitness account of the 1985 European Cup final at Heysel Stadium in Belgium, in which 38 spectators were killed. The class and social nature of the aggression becomes clear, as does the identity of the antagonists: police and team ownership. The decrepit stadiums, built for the working-class fans (or, rather, to imprison them) who attend the games and who presumably can expect no better, are themselves a contributing factor in such tragedies.

"When the fighting started, me and my mates ran to the back of the stand and jumped onto the roof of a hut to get out of the way. The roof just gave way and we fell straight through it.

There would never have been this outrage if the ground had been in a decent state. It would never have happened if the authorities had got their act together...

We didn't know anyone had died until half time, and people started walking out in disgust.

After the initial trouble everything calmed down. Some of the fans had put their banners over the fence at the front of the terraces. The police moved in and started tearing them down just for the sake of it. Then there was murder on again.

Now they are calling for national service to come back and all that crap. Then you can really kill people. Give them a rifle to do the job properly.

They treat you like animals — Liverpool Football Club have never given a fuck about their supporters. When we played in Paris last year they discouraged fans from going with horror stories about how bad the CRS was and so on...

Up our way football is the opiate of the people. When you've got nothing to do, and no money, it becomes the be-all and end-all.

You're treated like cattle. I used to go to away matches. In a car it's alright, but it's terrible if you go on the coaches, so I don't really bother now. If you step off the kerb you get a kicking. When I was 14 I got kicked by a police horse in the back of the head at Nottingham — it knocked me out".

Not surprisingly, a working-class youth often sees soccer hooliganism as an initial means of effecting change. The following document, as example, was published and distributed in France in the same year as the Heysel Stadium disaster.

THE EUROPE OF HOOLIGANS*
AND THE DEATH OF FOOTBALL

We are disgusted by the campaign of lies and encouragement of people to inform on each other presently being waged against football hooligans, and especially the supporters of Liverpool. As a matter of fact, during the summer of '81 in Liverpool, we met some of these supporters of LFC who had participated in the Toxteth riots; they became our friends (in such situations one makes friends easily). We won't stand seeing them insulted by petty journalist buffoons, nor by the hysterical crowd of all those who stuff themselves with their nauseating rumblings.

The Liverpool fans are in no way responsible for the 38 deaths at Heysel stadium in Brussels. The only ones responsible are the organizers of the sporting spectacle who pack the crowds into terraces. These structures are planned to hold passive crowds who content themselves with merely watching.

This policed cooping up is such that people can't even escape when they have to. On the 11th of May in Bradford, if there were so many deaths it was because the panicking spectators could not escape through the emergency exits; the stadium managers had blocked them in order to prevent people sneaking in! At Heysel, a shit of an employee refused to open an emergency gate opening onto the pitch for the panicking Italians. The cops pushed people back with truncheons to stop them seeking refuge on the pitch. A few seconds later, 38 died.

38 deaths — what is that? A lot more die on the roads each week-end, yet no one makes it a concern of the State! Because in this case it is a matter of the poor isolated in their tin cans. In Brussels it was a crowd; and the social system based on the manipulation of solitary

---

* Hooligans are not all neo-nazi skinheads, nor skinheads all neo-nazis.

crowds sees them escaping all control, even when they are herded like animals into caged enclosures. As even an Italian fan recognized: caged in as they were, it was inevitable (and, we would say, human) that the English supporters exploded and broke through the fences which separated them from others.

The English fans only wanted to explode a bit: a good fight with the others, even if they get together afterwards against the cops, and have fun in the town after the match.

That evening, the event didn't take place on the pitch but on the terraces: and for once it was a real event. This event was a measure of the nightmarish life which is imposed on us: crowd manipulation and police containment are the basis of the real world.

Unquestionably reality regained its place that evening on the 29th in Brussels. The nightmare which the spectacle exorcises in the sport show returned to the surface. "What should have been a celebration ended up as a tragedy," they lament. But what they lament above all is that the drama took place before the match. Their beautiful sporting event, broadcast in Eurovison, had simply been spoiled by reality! And if the match did finally take place, it was only for vulgar policing reasons (as usual, one could say, but the organizers were forced to say it: "What are we going to do with all these people?"). Besides, it was enough to listen, here and there, to the commentaries: the reflex of all these Pavlovian mongrels was to say that there wasn't enough cops that evening.

Today, all the European states use these 38 unfortunate victims to launch a hysterical counter-offensive against football hooligans; and the whole media of Europe lies about what really happened that evening in order to call for repression against the English fans. The worst scum are obviously the sports reporters: look at the articles of *L'Equipe* (French sports paper)! The sporting ideal has been irredeemably profaned! It's a good thing because the sporting ideal is shit.

Playing Dumb

Every week-end in Britain, proletarians go to matches in gangs, with the aim of smashing up, fighting and thus having fun. Really, they don't give a toss about sport. Nor do we. The so-called sporting event for them is only the pretext to get excited with the help of booze which, as well all know, warms the heart (on the other hand, it's well known that genuine sportsmen don't drink alcohol!). They are full of hate. Are there not enough reasons?! We too, we also hate. "We hate humans," said some years ago the youths of the Manchester United "Red Army". "I go to the matches only for one reason: to fight. It's an obsession. In London, in '84, 500 hooligans grouped together in a gang called the "Intercity Fraternity" in order to systematically raise hell at football events. After their devastating journey to Paris, one of them declared: "We wanted to do over the fascists of the (French) National Front, but your cops didn't give us the time to do it. So afterwards we only had one aim: to smash everything."

Everywhere in the world, the excitement produced and unsatisfied by the spectacle rebounds against it: in Dakar, Peking, Liverpool, Marseille, Tbilissi and elsewhere...

Simple minds find it absurd that people fight each other in this way for a football match. What they don't understand is that the match does not really matter. It's one occasion which is as good as any other: It's anyway more exciting to go to a football match or a rock concert than to a political demonstration. Fans often fight between themselves; and so what? After all what do they mean to each other? Nothing.

Who besides a leftist shit could be astonished that proletarians fight amongst each other for fun? Proletarians are united in nothing. They are completely separated. People's real misery is this absolute isolation organized in their daily life: usually this is expressed as indifference and sometimes as hostility. Only slaves of the spectacle and servants of the State are startled by the reality of misery, since it is them who are responsible for it.

It's from this reality that supercession begins. The same people who fight amongst themselves, depending which club they support, get together to fight the cops — like in the Saturday night punch-ups, or in the rivalry between gangs on housing estates. On the 29th, the English like the Italians, and even the Belgians constantly pelted the cops with missiles. Before the match, they also looted a jewellery and robbed some of the takings of the match. It's all this which enraged the European statesmen.

The Thatcher government decided to attack the football hooligans, after the rioters of '81 and the striking miners of '84 — because they are the same undisciplined proletarians who, crushed on one side, take revenge on the other. During the miners' strike, lots of hooligans fought on the side of the miners against the cops.

We share entirely the excitement of these hooligans who smash everything on their way and we are sickened by the measures announced against the British fans. The sanctions taken against the English clubs aim to prevent their supporters from going abroad. Within the country, they suffer maximum policing: ferocious judicial repression (recently some Chelsea hooligans were sentenced to between 6 months and five years in prison), reinforced police containment of the stadiums (obligatory ID cards for supporters, prohibition of alcohol consumption within or close or on the way to the stadiums, systematic video surveillance).

Whereas up till then football riots broke out most often during or at the end of the match, at Brussels they took place before, and they can even occur without a match, as happened in Doncaster on the 7th of March '85: it was two days after the tragic end of the long miners' strike. Several hundreds of supporters from the Sheffield team, allied with groups of young miners, went on the rampage in the centre of town (where there'd already been a riot of kids during the summer of '81) and ransacked the shops. The commentators, cops as well as journalists, had been very astonished by the fact that there'd been no match that day in Doncaster nor in the surroundings.

LONG LIVE THE FOOTBALL HOOLIGANS OF ENGLAND, DAKAR, PEKING, MARSEILLE, DETROIT, TBILISSI, AND OTHERS…!

LONG LIVE THE FOOTBALL CRAZIES!

Early June '85.

OS CANGACEIROS

This is a translation of a text distributed in France, in June.

3.
The Sporting Gaze

On the night of Klaus Croissant's extradition, the TV transmitted a football match in which France played to qualify for the world cup. Some hundreds of people demonstrated outside la Sante... twenty million people spent the evening glued to the screen. An explosion of popular joy when France won. Consternation and indignation of the illuminati over this scandalous indifference... nothing in this to deplore, but everything to analyze as the brute fact of a collective retaliation and of a refusal to participate in the recommended ideals, however enlightened.
— Jean Baudrillard In The Shadow of the Silent Majorities

It wasn't till a single sunless morning of early Indian summer that all my own gods proved me false: Risberg, Cicotte, Jackson, Weaver, Felsch, Gandil, Lefty Williams and a utility infielder whose name escapes me — wasn't it McMillen? The Black Sox were the Reds of that October and mine was the guilt of association.
And the charge was conspiracy.
Benedict Arnolds! Betrayers of American Boyhood, not to mention American Girlhood and American Womanhood and American Hoodhood...
I traded of the Risberg bat, so languid had I become, for a softball

Indecent Acts In A Public Place

model autographed only by Klee Brothers, who were giving such bats away with every suit of boy's clothing bought on the second floor. And flipped the program from that hot and magic Sunday when Cicotte was shutting out everybody forever, and a triumphant right-hander's wind had blown all the scorecards across home plate, into the troy Street gutter.
I guess that was one way of learning what Hustlertown, sooner or later teaches all its sandlot sprouts. "Everybody's out for The Buck. Even big-leaguers".
Even Swede Risberg.
— *Nelson Algren* Chicago: City on the Make

All sports are conducive to myth making, but none is more structured to make this so than baseball. Baseball is the most narrative of sports, requiring the creation of a text to complete it. Baseball's pauses, blandness and slow movement toward a dramatic climax, integrate the fan in the same way as the silences of a rhythmic piece of music or the repetition of a season of games leading up to the intensity of the playoffs. Its form is open-ended, allowing for unlimited creative possibilities and contradictions.

Baseball appeals to seemingly opposed worlds. Its mythic potential has made it particularly appealing to intellectuals and literati. They treat baseball with a reverence more often reserved for religion. At the same time, baseball lends itself to the realism of dialects, folk sayings and social concerns. It freezes another period in time like a strange behemoth locked in a glacier. Baseball arose at the same time as yellow journalism which found it not only conducive to narrative but easy to sensationalize. Sports journalism is still characterized by its repetitious use of themes whose banality itself becomes comforting.

It has often been pointed out that baseball was/is a means of spreading the propaganda of the corporate world. Its popularity as a sport grew among the rural and immigrant populations in the emerging urban centres. The first professional teams, formed by political machines, helped to mythologize expanding cities and their success stories as well as maintain, in myth, an America poised between two worlds: the urban and the rural, the old and the new, the corporate and the individual. The quantification of the sport supports the aspects in a baseball game that propagate myths appropriate to a corporate world. The player who makes the 'sacrifice play' is not punished with an official 'at bat' which would reduce his batting average; even the one who (in an appropriation of the Robin Hood myth) 'steals' for the good of the team is credited with a positive statistic.

Owners have capitalized on the nature of baseball by attempting to sell it as religion. They created a shrine at Cooperstown to which the fan can make a pilgrimage and pay homage before the mythical icons and idols to be founds there. That it is a complete fabrication — since Abner Doubleday did not invent the game nor were its origins in the U.S. — does not seem to matter.

The pervasiveness of mass media and the attempt to make sport a religious experience have not had the effect of silencing the noise of the fan. Baseball would never have become so popular if it did not allow an uncontrolled popular mythologizing as well. The fan does not simply absorb the values of the heroes placed before him , but counters the mythology and values of the official hero with myths of his own and by an increasing fascination with antiheroes of all sorts. Fans should be seen as lovers of myth and not as mere receptacles of corporate values. As a child will inevitably discover, such as in the beautiful passage from Nelson Algren quoted above, baseball, despite the efforts of owners and media, cannot help but reflect the underside of American life as well.

Watching a ballgame is to wonder if the institutionalized illegal tactic is being used. Is the pitcher throwing a spit ball? Has the player who dropped the easy pop-up taken too many drugs, just had another punch-up with the manager or taken a bribe to throw the game? Such tales have become mythic.

Baseball's open-ended time frame ("It's not over till it's over!") and space (the best hit ball is one that leaps over the outfield wall and into the world) can both hypothetically stretch into infinity, and, as ideological foundation, represent either a longing for westward expansion and manifest destiny or a nostalgia for the village green. It is this disparity we find when we go "to the heart of things (and) accept their myth" (Jean Giono *Ennemonde*). We see that much of American life that does not accord with the image of baseball that the owners may wish to present, is eventually revealed. The fan does quite naturally what I must struggle to do; see the essential meanings of sport as residing in its myth.

The world loves a hero, primarily because he can be used to fuel the fan's experience. Insofar as the athlete continues to do this he is granted whatever he wishes. (Showing that even the freedom to throw a game can be bought with a high enough wage.) By accepting official myths, the fan, often, helps to propel the hero to represent quite other values.

The athlete is granted a special status and pushed to exploit it. In a kind of spectacle where the fan's pleasure is mediated through the athlete and is based on the thrill of sexuality and violence (as acceptable and purchasable substitutes for sensuality and participation), then the more the athlete indulges the fan the greater the viewing pleasure. Athletes as an embodiment of acceptable virtues become increasingly outmoded. As the fan's representative within the sports world, the athlete can be pushed by him to step outside the law and live out the fan's fantasies, like the parents who push their child to do what they did not. Less reprehensibly, the fan is the immoral parent trying to push the hero to become an anti-hero. And when the athlete can no longer comply, then he is merely a bum and of no more use.

The emergence into prominence of the anti-hero has, perhaps, been obscured by the fact that to cheer for any athlete is somewhat decadent. The modern athlete is a union member who is pampered, granted special privilege, and paid millions of dollars a year to play a game — all the while acting like a prima donna. It is not surprising that he is held in high regard by the average fan.

Yet it is not surprising either, when the average fan trashes someone like 'the great Gretzky' (who, in his goodness and equanimity, is representative of an obsolete type of heroism) and shows more fascination for the star with the bad attitude; the one who cheats, loafs, carouses, womanizes, takes drugs and breaks the law. For it is the bad-attitude guy who not only tweaks his nose at the rules but at all the other heroes (the honest worker, the clean liver, etc.) and thus his own symbolic stature. It is he alone who attempts to go beyond the gratuities of symbolism, to exploit and indulge it in actual fact, living the fan's fantasy of a life of decadence and opulence.

The argument has been made that the star performer, noted for his indulgence in expensive commodities, serves as a reactionary promoter for consumerism, but this misses the point. His hedonism makes of the 'valuable' commodity its opposite; something easy to obtain and easily discarded. And, in being an individual caring only about his own indulgence, he once and for all proves the hero's insignificance.

A country goes wild when convicted game fixer Paulo Rossi scores the winning goal in soccer's World Cup — showing that one person can indeed do it all. The antihero supplants the hero in terms of significance (just ask the thousands of Italian families that named their new sons Paulo).

The sports fan is usually under attack from all quarters. His intense interest in sport is seen as an abrogation of family and other responsibilities and as an escape into a fantasy world.

Watching sports, however, is no more a lack of participation in 'life' than any of the other forms of involvement with the world that most would see as being open to them. It's no less 'real' because of its fantastic nature and, in fact, is a more intense form of (non)involvement than that recognizably possible in such things as politics, community and family.

The sporting gaze — that hypnotic integration into a world of heroes and myth — shows the fan's willingness to make dream life a part of the everyday world, and that that which is not boring will captivate him. It is not through political representation that the individual (though still separate from 'the action' to a degree) can, by his weekly cheering and booing, punish those he disapproves of or see a form of rough justice or immediate change imposed. It is through sports, not politics, that the individual finds a philosophical medium to discuss things that are relevant to his day to day life; things such as manhood, failure, and dealing with arbitrary authority. Sports is a vehicle through which he can express himself intellectually, emotionally and engagingly, and hence feel a daily bond with his fellows who do likewise (and who are in the majority) that he will not feel with his neighbours in a bedroom suburb or with a family only accessible by a long journey. Sports does not 'make up' for what is lacking in other parts of a person's life. It generates pleasure for what it is and is chosen above the others for what they are not.

Watching sports is making a choice for that which is simple but allows for any amount of intellectual involvement desired, that is dramatic, mythic, emotionally involving, active and fun. It is 'vicarious living' that overpowers 'life', the symbolism that can simply overcome all others. Rather than criticizing the sports fan for 'turning away from life', then, the logical criticism would be that if he derives so much pleasure from sports, that he doesn't seek to make it more intoxicating or to make the rest of the world more like it.

But what of the poor bugger who labours up 400 stairs with beer, pretzels, baseball hats and family in tow? Jammed into his seat, submissively accepting his blocked view, discomfort and putrid beer or, perhaps, experiencing the choreographed unity of 'the wave', do we see him as the embodiment of the dream of representation? Has he undergone a magical transformation where, through some act of symbiosis, his identity has become as one with his representative on the field, accepting them as the only legitimate actors? Is this a religious transcendence of experience where the individual is lifted beyond the day to day through his submission to something greater than himself? Is his cheering really a sign of his having been silenced? Is his presence a desire to participate in something that gets on the TV and in the papers (and is, thus, real)?

Whether as a corporation team, a state team or a city team, there is an apparent naturalness to representation, where the team is, seemingly, the embodiment of a collectivity. There is essentially no difference in this respect between teams in the U.S. and China. Americans moaning about the extreme propaganda effects that the Chinese seek to attain by winning at international sporting meets perform their own bit of national propaganda; their losing becomes a national moral victory.

Modern, high-performance sports are the children of political representation. Not surprisingly, sports critics and reformers reflect the colours of the political spectrum. They fight for the right to guide the direction of sport in the aim of the greater good, for 'black power', educational reform, colonial or anti-colonial attitudes, for liberal or conservative tax expenditures. They fight like crows over a carcass. Even when the resistance to state power by the fan is noted it is only seen as a localized resistance to some specific power. the naturalness of representation is never questioned. The high profile given to criticisms of professional North American sports leagues, because they are monopolies, obscures the fact that, even with more teams, representation is still supported and monopolization of that representation is still intact. The monopoly of leagues merely reflects the monopoly of representation.

The relationship between a sports team and the city whose name it bears on its chest is not a simple one of happy representation however. The team on the field battles as much for the acceptance of their own fans as against the other team. Like Ulysses, they return to town and must fight for the security and affections of their own people and land. Yet, in one sense, the fan allows for his representation because the city becomes the team's 'home turf' — an area laid claim to that it can exploit for its own gain — as much as it represents it.

Fans are fascinated with the corporate pimps known as sports owners, whose conviction ratio for crimes exceeds even that of their players. The lower the individual and the more they use their power to step on people the more they fascinate the fan. This is for the same varied and contradictory reasons that made Mario Puzo's *The Godfather* and its ilk best sellers as books and movies. It flows naturally from a recognition by the fan of the rough justice and gang-like qualities of the team. Baseball, as an example, was the child of machine politics and a continuation of its practice. The early sources of revenue established by the machines still exist: governments are fleeced for money and real estate and funds are generated by gambling. The process of the passing of ownership, from the openly corrupt politician (fearing the loss of middle-class support) to a 'respectable' corporate ownership of brewery owners and the like, has not fundamentally affected the nature of sports business but merely forced it to mask itself and become far more sophisticated and hidden than it was a hundred years ago. Pro sport still profits enormously from gambling and alcohol. Its use as a tax shelter directs, behind the scene, the activities and motives of teams. It affects the ages of players (i.e., players are assets whose value as a tax write-off diminishes over time), the salaries (higher salaries mean higher tax write-offs), the rapid turnover of teams, the quality of teams and the legitimacy of free agency.

The sports fan participates in the representations of pro sports because they allow him to create a more primitive form of representation. The fan enjoys the mediation of sports owners as crooks who function outside of the law (although they are actually integrated into the political process) because it is a part of their love of the sports team as a secret organization which functions behind public scrutiny, away from bureaucracy. Sports offers to the public an actual, and not simply mythic, underground economy that is open to all, a modicum of life away from surveillance.

Sports are about the jockeying of money, prizes and gambling. Sports increase circulation of money in a hidden and unregulated way which upends capital's normal monitoring mechanisms and distribution. Sports are the underground economy of office pools, betting, bribery, kickbacks, under-the-table payments and endorsements. Here is an illicit activity that the fan can participate in. To love professional sports is to affirm the secret codes and rituals of the tribe.

The tribal nature of the Mafia or the gang is an alternative to the corporate identity desired by sports and political representation. Tribalism can appear with its chants, masks and paint among the corporate body in the stands who witness a spectator event. It is an acceptance of the corporate identity of a tribe, of nomads, whether the tribe be one of skinheads, of a particular working-class gang or the fans of a team as a whole. While still a socially defined identity, it differs from that which reinforces political representation in that it is an identity formed by the public group themselves. The chanting of fans is the noise that attests to and expresses their strength. They appropriate all of the repetitions that seek to induce passive consumption; like the songs from beer commercials and rock music lyrics. That games begin with the national anthem attests to the fact that the music the fan himself creates is anti-representational.

Stadiums are built as monuments to a city or country and serve the aims of representation. They are rituals that confirm a city. Their other functions — such as use for political rallies — reinforces this. At the same time, they seek to contain the crowd. In extreme cases they can become prisons. That was the case during the overthrow of Allende in Chile and continues to be the case in soccer stadiums in Britain, where — because of the fear of autonomous noise and loss of social control — stadiums become prisons for hooligan gangs. The walls of stadiums ensure that a fee will be paid for entrance but also create the illusion of the city or state as separate and bounded. But while this is a place apart from the day to day, it is not a church. Its boundaries are accepted by fans because, unlike the rest of their daily life, they allow for a ritualistic and sacred space where the populace can create itself as a group. Only as a mob invading the city do fans emerge united. The crowd accepts its role as representative of the populace in a perverse way and collectively makes its appearance as outsiders to the city.

4.
Brute Strength

A little girl, just 18 months old, was claimed by her backers in London to be able to walk the length of the Mall (about a half mile) in 30 minutes. After the bets were laid, the toddler accomplished the task before the admiration of thousands in just 23 minutes.
It had long been a custom in the English countryside to have occasional 'smock races' for women. The winner would win a smock or loose dress of a thin fabric in which she was expected to pose after she was awarded it. In London in 1725 great numbers turned out for a four-mile race between four pregnant women. There were spectators and bettors on hand for wheelbarrow races, throwing contests, and hopping and jumping competitions…On a wager of 20 guineas, Lord Dunblain in 1683 was challenged to traverse 60 yards in 20 leaps… There were contests or races against time for dwarves, men with wooden legs, and other cripples. There were also prodigious feats of eating or drinking accomplished for a prize or to win a bet.

The reluctance of fighters to attack (and thereby risk a crippling riposte) made all of the Greek combative sports, particularly when done by experts, more akin to dancing than to bloody slugfests. A wrestling match or a boxing match might last days and be boring. It appears that wrestling and boxing may have been accompanied by music for that reason.
— *Richard D. Mandell* Sport: A Cultural History

Indecent Acts In A Public Place

The body, in Classical Greek sculpture, emerges for the first time in Western art as an object of beauty and contemplation; an ideal representation propagandizing particular values of manhood. The model for such a body was the Greek athlete.

The controlled body of Myron's discus-thrower twists unnaturally in mid-throw to create the balance and rhythm that give, through a static piece of bronze, an impression of the athlete's motion. What the work makes essential by its focus and composition is the control and beauty of the action and the actor. the discus-thrower's muscles are developed, but only to the point where grace and fluidity remain possible. The tension and relaxation of various muscles are detailed and give a sense of exertion, yet the face is passive, mask-like and remote. There is not yet, in fifth century B.C. work, the qualities of sensual pleasure and self-reflection evident in the subjects of Praxiteles and the sculptors of the fourth century.

Twenty-four centuries later, moviegoers witnessed an exhausted Sylvester Stallone stumble through the climactic match of the film *Rocky*. The lessons of composition from Greek sculpture are carried on, but not the images of the body or manhood. The kinesis is sensational and melodramatic; the flowing of blood and the puffing of eyes is detailed meticulously. Rocky, brain-scrambled, mumbles in a voice barely articulate to begin with. As an object of brute strength and overdeveloped muscles, he is an embodiment of the fortitude and qualities necessary to live out the American dream; to withstand beatings, pain, humiliation and punishment right up to the sentimental conclusion where boy gets girl.

Sculpture, of the sort produced by Myron, emerged following the nomadic Greek 'dark ages' and was coincident with the rise of the Olympic Games. Together they served as a representation and testing of the esteemed values of Greek culture and military might during the establishment of the powerful city-states.

In a similar way, ideals of the modern body emerged during the industrial revolution and the establishment of new relations of power. Little is known of the sports that preceded the Greek classical period except for those of the nobility, but in the modern West the emergence of new body ideals was coincident with the rise of new types of sport. These were quantified, high-performance, spectator sports, usually reserved for men, and they came to overwhelm folk forms of entertainment.

The ideal modern bodies that accompanied these changes were based on the assignation of certain values to either men or women. These values were supportive of the split between the sexes (man as worker, woman as homemaker and mother) that the development of wage labour and commodity production was based upon. The modern body was the product of a unique historical splitting between the sexes, and while the ideal images undergo changes, the sexualization of certain characteristics as either male or female remains.

For most of this century the athlete's body has been that of the male. At a time when sports have been generally a masculine pursuit, the male athlete's body — though in actuality usually battered and unhealthy — is a representation of strength and (sexual) power. Ideally it demonstrates brawn, size and the ability to do a workman's job — a sweating example of the struggle necessary for success; the absolute rightness of development and the strength needed for dealing with all comers. It is to be emulated by men and to be desired in a partner by women. In short, the ideological embodiment of the successful worker fantasized as hunter and warrior.

The male body is a denial, too, of its 'feminine' nature. Those elements of grace, beauty and the elegance of athleticism that can be (as in classical Greece) found to coexist with strength and power in the same body. The bifurcation between men and women takes on class characteristics. The activities reserved for women — the 'higher class' feminine cultural forms such as dance — are consistent with her role as sexless guardian of culture and the home.

Women can, if they so choose, assume the role of groupies. They can have surrogates of the sexuality and adventure reserved for men by performing the necessary function of maintaining the athlete's image as a sexual star by giving it an assumed substance. Or they can perform the service of being a bargaining chip when a team is courting the big player. All one needs to qualify as a nude model in *Penthouse* or *Playboy* magazine is to have been the mistress or wife of a Wade Boggs or Jake LaMotta.

The female weightlifter who ignores the apartheid between male and female body images — insofar as they reflect particular social values — looks absurd with her bulging muscles to an eye accustomed to very specific body dimensions. Yet, in her grasping to encompass the qualities she has been denied, she is far from absurd. In fact, as the proliferation of women wrestlers indicates (the new woman packaged in a new genre of sexual titillation), she is cheered.

What a sculpture like Myron's does make ridiculous is the anthropologist who attempts to argue that modern sports are merely a continuation of men's historic and innate role as hunter/warrior/worker (the lower class complement to women). This ignores the historically 'feminine' nature (in today's cultural terms) of the male athlete. The obvious conclusion to be drawn from this is that body images and the sexuality they represent are not historical constants, and, in that they establish an oppositional sexual polarity, are in fact, anti-sexual.

The combining of dance and strength in a case like Greek boxing (see opening quote) does not point to either an historic novelty or an epitome of physical realization. The same elements can still exist together in modern boxing. This can be seen in the distinction between 'boxers' and 'sluggers' — which are not mutually exclusive characteristics. Witness former champion Muhammed Ali ('floating like a butterfly') who has made the otherwise curious comment that what people fail to realize about boxing is that you don't have to get hurt. And interestingly — following the tendency to see these as class distinguishers — while boxing has appealed to blacks as an underclass with few options, using them generally as cannon fodder for entertainment (i.e., thousands participate at an early age looking for a way of 'making it', while only a very few actually live out the fantasy), they have not become the 'lower class' within the sport. The slow shuffling pug, barroom-type fighter is almost always white.

The athlete's body is one of the primary commodities in the business of sport. As an actual entity it is bought, sold and traded between teams. But it is sold to the public as well, as reified image of something scarce and exclusive, the physical incarnation of certain virtues. As such, the athlete's body has become purchasable — for those willing to undertake the necessary regimen — as a compensation for the non-democratic nature of modern sports. To own an athletic body is to attain a substitute for what pro sports denies its spectators: the joy of participation and the sensuality of movement. This is fundamentally different from the Greek ideal, which represented accessibility, participation and pleasure.

As feminism has filtered down to a popular level, the male — confronted with a form of athletic participation based on the sexual in both the narrowest and broadest senses (i.e., the qualities associated with the male in a particular historical division) — has found it acceptable to express his desire for sensuality by such actions as condemning the aggressive values of male athletics and an increased personal participation.

In order for the athlete to retain his specialized function as model of body image, some changes have begun to occur. The athlete's body is increasingly hidden by plastic and synthetic uniforms to disguise its decrepit physical condition (and masculine nature) in order to present itself as an image (partially feminine) of health and vigour. Athletes promote participation and speak out against drugs and alcohol while efforts are made to curtail such male excesses as hockey violence.

In the same vein, females (now participating to a greater degree as well) increasingly work to establish women's professional sports along the same lines as those for men. This means that they too can have specialized athletic models as they seek to attain some of the 'masculine' qualities (e.g., physical power) denied them.

Memberships at gyms, sports equipment, books and a variety of other commodities are profitable business items. Even simple activities (like 'catch' in the park) that can be engaged in by all, and done only for the urge to participate in some form of physical activity, become commodity-intensive. Expensive shoes, gym suits and other paraphernalia become necessary items. Their marketing has required pro sports to change as it has in order to protect its role in the colonization of the body.

The sports that both men and women participate in are, largely, individual sports. (Team sports, as the selling of the athletic men's society, remains dominated by small numbers of males and primarily in the business of selling sex and violence.) Racquet sports and golf allow women the development of strength and men of grace. But they lend themselves, too, to a social situation characterized by a high degree of commodity consumption; from the draping of tanned and hipless bodies with fashionable uniforms (sports fashion itself being a mediated item playing on the nostalgia for sensuality and athleticism) to the requiring of exclusive grounds (e.g., private clubs with fees) and one's own pro.

Squash, where one can meet new business clients, is valued over playing catch in the backyard for the fun of it. A tanning salon is essential for the look that a sport played in the park for pleasure and fresh air cannot guarantee. And the look is all-important. The image of the athlete as exceptional, a specialist, gives the corporate purchaser the satisfaction of seeming to be different while remaining the same as everyone else. Uniformed at work and play, with or without clothes. Jogging and other sports are, for young urban professionals, essentially no different than their obsession with cocaine and other recreational drugs. It is a distorted hedonism that merely confirms their position as consumers *par excellence* (that the syndicate loves) and that eventually sickens them. Their obsessiveness is a model for the corporate go-getter in all fields. The useless repetition of exercise binds the individual to the ideology of a programme as a synthetic drug substitute for the intoxication of sport.

Even as the hierarchy between male and female is erased, new class distinctions emerge that combat the democratic accessibility of the symbolism of the athlete's body. The new upper class can not only own an athletic body; it can own an athlete. To have one's own pro is to integrate a purchasable, and thus unequalizing, pedagogical element, where skill is improved in accordance with cash outlay. 'Community-owned' pro teams with multiple shared owners are on the increase. And ownership of the view of athletes — with private seats or boxes — is still a nice tax write-off.

The modern model for a sport that indicates social position is, of course, horse racing. But its status diminished as it became too obviously capitalistic, and thus crass.

Horse racing has been left in large measure to the con-man, quick-buck artist and shyster; being purely capitalist it was no longer so symbolic of the aristocracy and upper classes.

Horse racing is gambling and therefore based on the desire (in the spirit of the aristocrat) to cheat the world of work. This is to be done by accumulating capital; by being rich. To be one of those who "preach the dignity of labour, while taking care themselves to remain undignified in this respect" (Bertrand Russell *In Praise of Idleness*). It is, thus, not a challenge to the world of work.

Insofar as it is based on winning, horse racing is a gamble not only for the bettor but also for the owner, who invests in a horse as he/she would the stock market; not to mention the jockeys and trainers whose incomes ride directly on a horse's accomplishments.

This has led horse racing to institutionalize cheating and the unsavoury tactic. Examples abound. A horse's training times are falsified — in the hope that the odds placed against it will increase — by having it run slower than it can in training laps. An injury is feigned so that a horse may be moved to a lower class of race (i.e., against weaker competition) without its being claimed and thus 'steal' a purse.

The sharp owner can make money by clever and fast dealings that utilize other unethical business tactics. In one such practice, a horse (which, like a work of art, is only so much capital invested, whose value is based on its apparent scarcity) can have its value artificially inflated or reduced. One way this occurs is by selling some of the offspring of a particular horse to an unknown agent — in reality a friend or family member — at a highly overvalued price in the hope of driving up the price on remaining stock.

With horse racing losing its status as the 'sport of kings', it is to other sports that the new corporate executives turn to show their position. It is no longer the purchase of an animal that signifies one's class to the world, it is the purchase of the athlete's body in fact.

Modern spectator sport sees the emergence of the athlete as commodity. He is both employee and product; a resource that is usable until his value depreciates, at which point he is discarded. As a commodity, the athlete becomes like other commodities, distinguishable (from the horse or racing car) only symbolically. But in order for this to happen there has necessarily been a transference of status and related treatment from the animal to the athlete. This could only occur because the animals used in sports, by a process of breeding and use, have long since ceased to be anything but a caricature of actual animals. They, in turn, are becoming more machinelike.

Brute Strength

The beauty of the power of the horse in the wild is undeniable, but horse racing, with its use of horses that are often so ill that they must be supported with drugs in order to complete a race, trades only on the memory of that beauty and a nostalgia for the freedom of riding. Likewise, the illusion of the athlete as 'sexual animal', barely tamed, helps us to forget the fact that he is more like a domestic pet.

The athlete, like the animal, is bought, sold and traded as a commodity. He is bred bigger, better and stronger with drugs such as steroids and with increased training beginning with a selective process at an earlier age. Like the racehorse that is susceptible to injury because of the concussive impact of a heavy body on ultra thin legs, the athlete is increasingly injury-prone. While this trend is partly due to the demands for greater quantitative achievement (higher, faster, stronger) and the apparent need for owners to produce winners, the athlete is complicit in his own downfall when he willingly accepts such treatment for financial gain (though often out of financial necessity).

The claim has been made that sports are primarily male because they are played on areas appropriate to the male body. But they are suitable only for the maladapted body. Such is the case with the racehorse, which must be trained over a long period of time to ignore the dictates of its own body and run the unnatural distance of one and a quarter miles. (When in a field, a horse will race with its peers for 100 to 200 yards and then stop, winded). Like the racehorse who has the nerves in its legs cut, the athlete is pressured to risk extreme injury by playing on a frozen (i.e., already injured) knee or leg. And the fan, demanding greater achievement, grants athletes about the same amount of sympathy as he does cocks at a cockfight. The uniform that hides the athlete's maleness, and his increasingly worked-over body, must now hide his human features as well.

The objectification of the athlete now spreads to recreational athletes as well. Steroid use is on the increase for 'experimentation with body image', as is plastic surgery. The body is becoming a cybernetic system, pointing to an increase of bionics, drugs, scientific experimentation and finally the destruction of the biological body.

The process of turning the human body into an animal and then a machine makes sports antithetical to an appreciation of the human body, and those who seek to destroy their body the most logical proponents of modern trends. Such is the case with the anorexic who seeks to will away the body altogether; an affliction of both males and females. The compulsive jogger undergoes the same physical effects as the anorexic by using up all reserves of body fat and then burning muscle tissue. Surely, 'no pain no gain', the aphorism utilized by even casual athletes, has to be one of the most despairing comments ever issued as a truism about the human body or human aspirations.

The 'pedestrian' events (see opening quote) organized by shady entrepreneurs to make quick money and exploit the anarchy of gambling, still reflect the qualities of peasant festival. Particularly, equal participation for males and females of all ages and in all physical conditions whose chief aim in participating was to have fun. One can see modern similarities in certain self-regulated, non-ideological activities that do not attempt to control representation and are not defined by commodification. They can be as simple as the intelligent gang of men, women and children that plays together for an afternoon of games to foster any types of relationships that they choose, in a direct and non-abstract way. It does not require the educated and indoctrinated to experience the space and time of ritual; the exuberance that sports psychologists can't direct. But the urge to overcome the lack of these qualities in the modern world has, unfortunately, been largely channelled by a feminism which buys the symbolism of pro sports and body images. Change is equated with leaving one social class for another; change that requires leaders and increased consumption. Improvement is measured by increasing numbers owning athletic bodies, or athletes, or becoming a commodity sold to the public. Change, filtered through the feminism of *Ms* magazines and Jane Fondas, has accelerated a process of body hate and mechanization.

The commodification of the body has, literally, destroyed it. The game is an extension of the body, and must be increasingly seen as characterized by it pathology. Like the body of the athlete fed on synthetic substances, it is increasingly repugnant.

With its aesthetic and abstract goals, modern sports become increasingly like the ideologically based athletics of track and field, the Olympics (which co-opts and alters the Greek ideal) or even Nazi athletics. It shows a commitment to high-performance sports which destroy the body, are anti-pleasure and exclusive, and are based on a drug-like addiction to repetition. This applies equally to the recreational athlete, since the degree of formality is not important but the degree of rationalization is. Understandably women, and growing numbers of men, may not be interested in the male fantasies of team sports, but the increasing attention given to high-performance, individual sports, undermines the methods of resistance that the sports fan has developed through watching team sports. The values which the body promotes have been challenged, but not its commodification. The further sport goes towards a justification of abstractions and ideology — becoming 'high art' — the more it inhibits itself from remaining a base for the expression of public goals and myths, and the less popular it becomes. As demonstrated by the Soviet athlete, the sole recourse for a participant who wants to resist the commitment required by an ideologically based athletics is to assert the alternative ideology of self by demanding star treatment.

It is too simplistic however, to see a simple option for the future between activities like jogging and the viewing of professional team sports. The promotion of individual or non-spectator sports does not in itself provide any alternative to modern sports when they are still defined by commodification and deny the possibility of a freedom from an officially defined identity. The future is not simply a choice between doing and watching. If the growth and popularity of modern sports shows anything, it is the enormous pleasure that people find in looking.

5.
The End of Sport

The participation of fans and athletes strengthens the business of pro sports. But it does not indicate that viewers have been manipulated into the passive consumption of a spectacle that silences them and enhances social harmony, or that athletes are simply mindless models of masculinity and corporate values. The behaviour of fans and athletes is too often identified with the façade of moralism and social order that sports administrators claim to represent and instil. The active, playful behaviour of those who participate in sports generally goes unnoticed. In fact, it is this play — characterized by its festive and creative acts that challenge what infringes on social and moral autonomy — that organized sports seeks to control in order to construct itself as a commodity. It is because sports mimics festival — as a special realm set apart from the day to day where this sort of play rules — that it is so popular.

A struggle always exists between fans and athletes on the one side and those who control sports. Participants use sport as a medium of pleasure, hedonism, exuberance and sedition. Those who manage sports present a mask of strict morality while attempting to transform the wants of the participants into demands for drugs, prostitution and gambling. This conflict can be seen in the nature of the fraternity that develops between the men who come together as athletes.

The fraternity of athletes develops as a totemic men's society; an orgiastic community, exclusively for men and ritually bound together, whose solidarity allows them to transgress moral and social norms. The development of the men's society is systematically retarded by the business of sports that attempts to sell it as a spectacle of titillation. It encourages the rebelliousness of this society when it is sensational and nothing more. Membership in the men's society is sold to the fan as a means of overcoming his exclusion from being a player. Although the fan engages in this prostitution he uses it to brutalize athletes for their involvement — the john beating up the hooker.

Sports teams embody the qualities of the illegal groupings that manifest themselves outside the law. A team is subject to both those who create it as a gang, without a hierarchy of power, directed against authority and its laws, and those who wish to structure it as a corporately run syndicate whose business is the illegal commodity. It is this authority, functioning within sports, that ensures that the players on teams, as a tactic of resistance, must retain their adolescent and gang-like features. Fans promote the oppositional nature of the gang in the face of attempts to make its qualities merely cathartic and dramatic, and confined by the arena.

The fan is not a submissive receptacle of the propagandizing narrative of sports. The fan's gaze, though intense, is active. Fans do accept certain mediation when to do so furthers their own purposes and pleasure. Cheering a supposedly 'bad boy' owner is parallel to the experience of a peasantry that aids the mafia because it attacks an arbitrary outside authority. Sports is, for its viewers, a vehicle of expression and fantasy. They counter official mythology

The End of Sport

with myths and anti-heroes of their own. Sports becomes a philosophical medium for discussion and, as such, retains a relevancy to people's lives.

That sports is not a passive activity has been occasionally noted, but in a selective way, such as with the description of the rebellion of fans as opposition to a particular form of political representation. This does not capture how the entirety of sports is a realm of challenge for its participants, who actively create their own behaviour. When people come together at a stadium or arena, it does not serve as a church or a place of submission to some abstraction beyond their control. It is a time and space where the group creates itself with its own voice and its own rituals.

Commercial sport has been forced to adapt to retain its legitimacy and control. Its primary commodity continues to be the athlete, made so by being first transformed into an animal and then a machine. His body has always been symbolic, throughout this process, of the values which reinforced commodification, wage labour and social stratification. The rejection of the sexual apartheid of values, and the purchase of these in the stead of involvement, has led to an intensification of commodification and the idealization of the body. The attainment of such a body has increasingly become recognition of consumer ability and class.

The athletic body and sports reflect each other. The body is increasingly characterized by anorexia, sickness and pain. Sports offers ideality, addictive repetition, and performance in synthetic and controlled environments. Finally, the body is being cast off altogether as an irrelevancy. Current trends, such as mechanization and miniaturization will certainly continue. Like the game of golf you play on a computer, the aim seems to be to make play itself a simulation of play.

Since the institution of sports and play-as-festival are not equivalent, there is no reason to conclude that autonomous play is confined to sports, or that play, with its seditious and liberating qualities, will not persist. Given the way that sports are used, their immense popularity can be seen as evidence that play is central to people's lives. It is of obvious importance to them and, perhaps, their primary means for creative expression and to exert an autonomous will. It's not news (at least not to some) that, besides sports, playfulness invades other areas of people's lives (such as work), and with similar effect. Nor is it a surprise that other social groupings function to similar purposes as sports teams. It may only be that it is not so readily apparent because it is organized sports that parodies the qualities of play in order to create an arena in which play can be controlled and commodified. But the point is, that if people increasingly begin to ignore the crippled body of modern sports (as it continues to attempt to restrict autonomous play and introduce new forms of leisure entertainment), that we should not conclude that play itself has diminished. Rather, it is only an indication that we must look elsewhere — to independent activities and new forms of contestation — to find it.

Select Bibliography

Select Bibliography

- Algren, Nelson. *Chicago: City On The Make*. New York: McGraw-Hill, 1983.

- Attali, Jacques. *Noise. The Political Economy Of Music. Theory And History Of Literature. Vol. 16*, trans. Brian Massumi. Minneapolis: University Of Minnesota Press, 1985.

- Barnes, LaVerne. *The Plastic Orgasm*. Toronto: McClelland & Stewart Ltd., 1971.

- Baudrillard, Jean. *In The Shadow Of The Silent Majorities Or The End Of The Social And other Essays*, trans. Paul Foss, John Johnston and Paul Patton. New York: Semiotext(e) Foreign Agents Series, 1983.

- Bloch, H.A. and Arthur Niederhoffer. *The Gang: A Study In Adolescent Behaviour*. New York: Philosophical Library, 1958.

- Brasch, R. *How Did Sports Begin? A Look At The Origins Of Man At Play*. New York: Davis McKay Company Ltd., 1970.

- Brown, Norman O. *Love's Body*. New York: Vintage Books, 1966.

- Cabins, Lucius. "Drugs: A Corrosive Social Cement". Processed World 11 (Summer, 1984): 52-63

- Campbell, Joseph. *The Masks Of God: Primitive Mythology*. New York: The Viking Press, 1970.

- Cawelti, John G. "The New Mythology Of Crime". Boundary 2 Vol. 3, no. 2 (Winter, 1975): 325-358

- Cohen, Marvin. *Baseball The Beautiful. Decoding The Diamond*. New York: Links Books, 1974.

- Cosell, Howard and Peter Bonaventure. *I Never Played The Game*. New York: William Morrow and Company Inc., 1985.

- Deleuze, Gilles and Felix Guattari. *Nomadology: The War Machine*, trans. Brian Massumi. New York: Semiotext(e) Foreign Agents Series, 1986.

- Dickey, Glenn. *The Jock Empire*. Radnor, Penn.:Chilton Book Co., 1974.

- Freud Sigmund. "Totem And Taboo". *The Basic Writings Of Sigmund Freud*, ed. and trans. A.A. Brill. New York: The Modern Library, 1938: 807-930

- Gardner, Paul. *Nice Guys Finish Last. Sport And American Life*. New York: Universe Books, 1975.

- Gladman, Jerry. "Bad Sports". Toronto Sun (Mar. 22, 1987): 14-15

- Gruneau, Richard B., ed. *Popular Cultures And Political Practices*. Toronto: Garamond Press, 1988.

- Hagedorn, John with Perry Macon. *People And Folks. Gangs Crime And The Underclass In A Rustbelt City*. Chicago: Lake View Press, 1988.

- Hamil, Pete. "Give Baseball A Chance". Village Voice (Oct. 28, 1986): 10

Select Bibliography

- *The Odyssey of Homer*, trans. Richard Lattimore. New York: Harper Torchbook, 1968.
- Illich, Ivan. *H2O And The Waters Of Forgetfulness. Reflections On The Historicity Of 'Stuff'*. Dallas: Dallas Institute of Humanities and Culture, 1985.
- Illich, Ivan and Berry Sanders. *The Alphabetization Of The Popular Mind*. San Francisco: North Point Press, 1988.
- Kidd, Bruce and John Macfarlane. *The Death Of Hockey*. Toronto: New Press, 1972.
- Levine, Peter. *A.G. Spalding And The Rise Of Baseball. The Promise Of American Sport*. Oxford: Oxford University Press, 1985.
- Lipsyte, Robert. *Sportsworld: An American Dreamworld*. New York: Quadrangle Books, 1977.
- Ludwig, Jack. *Games Of Fear And Winning. Sports With An Inside View*. Toronto: Doubleday, 1976.
- Mandell, Richard D. *Sport: A Cultural History*. New York: Columbia University Press, 1984.
- Millman, Joel. "Miami Blitz". Mother Jones Vol. 11, no. 9 (December, 1986): 36-42, 46-50
- Opie, Iona and Peter. *Children's Games In Street And Playground*. Oxford: Oxford University Press, 1969.
- Parrish, Bernie. *They Call It A Game*. New York: The Dial Press, 1971.
- *Rebel Violence V. Hierarchical Violence. A Chronology Of Anti-State Violence Ob The UK Mainland. July 1985 - May 1986*. London: B.M. Combustion, 1986.
- Sarick, Lila. "Steroids crafting new body language for recreational athletes". Globe & Mail (Mar. 27, 1989): 12
- Scott, Jack. *The Athletic Revolution*. New York: The Free Press, 1971.
- Short, James F. and Albert K. Cohen. "Gang". Collier's

Encyclopedia, Vol. 10: 565-567

- Surface, Bill. *The Track. A Day In The Life Of Belmont Park*. New York: Macmillan, 1976.
- Vincent, Ted. *Mudville's Revenge. The Rise And Fall Of American Sport*. New York: Seaview Books, 1981.
- Vogel, Harold L. *Entertainment Industry Economics. A Guide For Financial Analysis*. Cambridge: Cambridge University Press, 1986.

www.ingramcontent.com/pod-product-compliance
Lightning Source LLC
Chambersburg PA
CBHW021122080526
44587CB00010B/607